Writing Serial Fiction In the Real World 2.0

A Simple Guide to Writing and Publishing Episodic Stories Everywhere, For Profit

While every precaution has been taken in the preparation of this book, the publisher assumes no responsibility for errors or omissions, or for damages resulting from the use of the information contained herein.

WRITING SERIAL FICTION IN THE REAL WORLD 2.0

First edition. April 23, 2021.

ISBN: 979-8201180942

Written by Dr. Robert C. Worstell.

Table of Contents

To all our many devoted and loyal fans:

We write and publish these stories <u>only</u> for you.

(Be sure to get your bonuses at the end of the story...)

Update: For You, I Took This Back To Evergreen Principles That Won't Change.

Originally, I wrote this considering more people would find it on Amazon, so it was tailored to that market.

Then you went and bought it years later, and I knew it needed to be updated and expanded. So I did.

Since I first wrote it, I've discovered and witnessed that Amazon has become the new author's graveyard for fiction ebooks. That platform is super-saturated and almost impossible to succeed at. So I generally avoid recommending anything that is specific to their ebook outlet. (Paperbacks, particularly non-fiction, are a completely different story – but that's another book.)

Going through this book to remove any platform-specific data was one thing. I mention below that I've now spent three years writing fiction and testing all the advice I'd published before. That meant I could also remove advice that was found unworkable.

And I added a big section on cliff-hangers, which is essential for writing serials.

You're welcome.

And you can now find an enlarged Bibliography and lots of links to books that that cover what I discovered since.

Also, gratis.

Let me get out of your way, then.

INTRODUCTION: THIS EPISODE IS BROUGHT TO YOU BY...

THE REASON I WROTE this for you was because I couldn't find a decent ebook anywhere for this subject. The two I could find there were pathetic (and if you think this one is another, perhaps you should be writing your own. Jump right in, the water's fine...)

So I went out on the Internet and assembled all the research I could to see what and how this subject worked, if it did or not.

Then I compared what I'd learned with what I already knew – and wrote it up for you so you could use it.

Finally, I tested this for three years to improve my craft. And so I now update all my earlier text.

I don't pretend to know anything about this subject other than what you see here. So there.

I have now published several hundred fiction books, and far more non-fiction, so I know how to research and edit and publish. Writing is an endless journey that takes you far, but you never see its end. As you apply yourself, as you push your own envelope, then you improve and find more areas to expand into.

Just to be transparent, my work has been in non-fiction (mostly.) And I got back into studying story structure and plotting, etc. Because the better selling non-fiction works were built on either a narrative, or the "Big Idea" (which is really a collection of short narratives built on the same theme.)

You'll see later in this book my concept for a business plan you can use. How that will work for you is exactly as you understand what I wrote here, as you understand the authors I quoted and linked to, and as you test and apply this data in your own personal scene.

I think it can be made to work, despite all the naysayers we'll encounter soon enough.

It's up to you do decide whether you want to continue on and dive deep into the bottomless pool of your own creativity to surface with new ideas and applications.

Our target is that tiny school of small fish called serials.

Let's see how they're biting today...

PART ONE - WHY SERIALS? WHY NOW?

WRITING SERIAL FICTION SUCCESSFULLY ISN'T FOR THE FAINT OF HEART

THE ETERNAL QUESTION for this book is: "Can we write profitable serials for print or ebooks?"

While some writers work at writing for art's sake, the bulk of this would like some monetary gain as well as the fame and glory.

There are two schools of thought and opinion about publishing books and stories online. One school is writing the novel or longish non-fiction work, the other is writing short stories.

(**Note:** Most of this book was originally written to deal with ebooks, as that is the current fad. Under the radar is print books, which continue to far out-sell ebooks in both units and royalties to authors. The following data applies to both, but most of the examples are written for ebooks.)

A recurring statistical conclusion is that only 300- and 400-page books are making any "real money". Smashwords' founder, Mark Coker, has been releasing his annual reports for some time, based on his own internal number-crunching. They found the trend that longer ebooks sold better and longer than shorter ebooks. He was also the first to find that the $3.99 price range was best for fiction. (The second best price is $2.99.) Unfortunately, Amazon accepts very few ebooks from

Smashwords for their catalog. So any Amazon book data was missing - until this year.

In one of their last reports before going private, Author Earnings released their own number-crunching results based on bot-scrapes of Amazon's site and found the same thing. (But you'll have to check this out on Archives.org Wayback Machine, since they pulled down their site as well – link in Bibilograhy.)

(**Note:** Coker also noted that several of his top sellers were box sets, meaning several books cobbled together. His high average was about 112,000 words, which equates roughly to 450 pages. So this finding may need review.)

What AE also found, incidentally, that most ebook authors didn't sell well, and most ebooks didn't sell well. Amazon has rightly earned the name of "author graveyard." AE says they found just 1600 authors (that's *total*) earning a living wage from Amazon, which is over $50K per year. The author community on Amazon speculates that there may be over 500,000 authors publishing there according to Amazon's Author Rank numbers - but only authors that ever sold anything are counted. (Yes, there are self-published authors on Amazon who have never sold anything. Imagine that.)

Still, ebooks are a multi-billion dollar industry, and Amazon has 70% of that market per AE. It shows no real sign of disappearing anytime soon. Despite how they treat new authors.

Now, not to disappoint you, there are holes in these statistics. (As Mark Twain was credited: "There are lies, damned lies, and statistics.")

Per AE, Amazon's total sales are just that. They aren't weighted by how many books of a certain page-length exist for sale in any genre or category.

Amazon doesn't categorize their books by length, generally. The bestselling category according to AE is Romance and there are nearly 384,000 Romance Kindle books.

If you visit K-Lytics.com and get a copy of their updated seminars on short reads and short stories, you'll have the most accurate analysis of what is happening on Amazon ebooks according to page-length.

For example, at this writing there are just under 59,000 Romance ShortRead ebooks. Under 3,000 of these are less than 12 pages. A 100,000 to one ratio. What's pointed out in the K-lytics seminar is that while short reads sell less than longer books, they sell at a much greater per-page income. This figures into some very interesting applications...

THE SWEET SPOT FOR SERIALS

WHILE BOTH AMAZON AND Itunes have a 2500-word minimum for accepting any book is 2500 words, K-lytics points to ebooks in the 100 -page range as having probably the best sales per page. With 250 words per page, this brings your content up to novelette or novella range (about 25,000 words). However, you'll see below that it's faster to write shorter works of about 6,000 words and then cobble them into longer works – hint.

Note: If you want to scratch what follows on a spreadsheet or pad of paper as I lay this out, you might be able to poke holes in this or work out your own best plan...

If you were able to write 2,000 words a day, as Stephen King was doing when he wrote his "On Writing", and you take Amazon's estimate of 250 words per page, that's four pages per day. It would take you approximately 75 days to write a first draft for a 300-page book. At 5 days per week, this would then be 15 weeks, or over a third of a year. With editing and re-writes, you'd add to this. Figure 90 days on average, with getting the cover made, proofing, etc. That doesn't take into account multiple drafts some authors use – and so the expected output of 300 page books is about two per year. (And that is self-publishing. Traditional publishing adds a year to produce a book like that – *after* it's written and submitted.)

(**Warning**: we are going into Amazon-centric jungle of their particular book royalties. Barnes & Noble now gives a flat 70% royalty for any ebook, regardless of length. Kobo and the others are slightly different. Google books is far worse than Amazon.)

Figure that you could conceivably crank out two 300-page books a year. Your best price being $3.99, and selling one book per day, at a 70%

royalty, this would make you just over $2100 per year after they were both published as Amazon ebooks.

If you are writing serials (and have an incredible work-ethic as well as a limitless imagination to bring you new ideas) you could conceivably crank out two 6,000 word stories a week or about 25 stories a year.

Short shorts (2500 words) are usually sold at .99 each. At that level, Amazon only grants you 35% royalty. 25 books would then give you over $3100 annually (at one sale per day, our standard.)

Taking a $2.99 sales point for your collecting your short reads into "boxed sets", you'd earn a 70% royalty. Figuring that you collect 8 episodes into a collection and market that as a "season" the years production would give you 3 such collections and nearly another $2300. But you'd also be able to combine those collections into bigger collections (called "boxed sets") at a $3.99 price point, giving you another $1,000. Total would be about $6400 per year.

Which is a better use of your writing time? Two books a year for $2100, or 25 books with collections for $6400? Same amount of time. Different incomes.

To make your $50K income, you either produce 2 books a year for 23 years, or 25 ShortReads a year for nearly 8 years. Your choice. (Yes, you can do *much* better than this with effective marketing.)

Now, all that said, there is no real reason to sell any ebook below $2.99, no matter how short. You'll find authors who give their first three novels away for .99 on special offers, and then rake in a six-figure income as they buy the other two novels in that series. Your first works are giving the audience a taste. You'll see later how this develops their taste buds into a craving for your work as you apply some classic writing strategies of serials and cliffhangers.

OK, all that above tends to get us all bleary-eyed over numbers and potential earnings.

Your mileage may vary - and less than 100,000 Kindle ebooks (out of well over 3 million) sell more than 1 per day, so this is an optimistic view of potential income. The point is that there is potential here despite these statistics, if possibly inspired by them.

But next: Is it still true that serials are dead - and doesn't that make all this a worthless mental exercise?

WHERE DID ALL THE SERIALS GO?

THEY ARE STILL THERE – just in different formats and media...

Most of the books on Serials cover how Charles Dickens and other early authors made their living publishing in periodicals, and then publishing books based on those installments. However, it's just not done that way anymore. And I cover that history of the serial in the Appendix. From reading that, you might think serials had become extinct as a species. Hardly.

After TV and movies started up, periodicals in print moved started shifting their focus from original fiction over to information and "news". What you see these days in magazines devoted to entertainment is more entertainment reportage on celebrities than fiction stories. Newspapers are only filled with ~~salacious gossip~~ "news". Tabloids are somewhere in between.

Some serialized fiction continued, though. In 1984, Tom Wolfe's "Bonfire of the Vanities" ran in 27 parts in Rolling Stone, where Wolfe was paid around $200,000 for his stories. Later, he heavily revised those articles in creating the standalone novel.

Most of Malcolm Gladwell's books were first published as magazine articles, and later cobbled together into huge hardbacks.

Stephen King tried serializing "The Plant" in 2000, and Michael Faber allowed the Guardian to serialize his "Crimson Petal and the White."

Online, fan fiction has risen in popularity on sites such as FanFiction.net. They attract more readers from the original movies, often being able to transfer their work to print or e-books.

More commonly, you'll see work published for free on web-based communities such as Fictionpress.com and Wattpad. Reportedly these books receive as many readers as successfully published novels, some receiving the same reader numbers as NYT bestsellers.

Of course free doesn't mean profitable, unless you can get those readers to follow you to a paid service.

And I have found in this research that a few people who are making serials are exclusive to Amazon. But that model is tricky, and not well known.

But that's why you're reading this - to see if they can be made to work. It's the question of if you can master this format and make it work for you.

Next, we dive into how the successful ones are really created - if you're up to it...

PART TWO - HOW TO ROLL YOUR OWN SERIAL AND NOT BURN YOUR FINGERS

BUILDING SERIALS IS A DIFFERENT TOOLSET, BUT THE SAME TOOLS.

A STORY IS A STORY is a story. No matter how short, they all tell it the same way.

This was the conclusion that resulted when I compared the most common and popular plotting techniques with each other.

If you take the Ancient Greek's 3-Act play, then add in our modern versions, such as Blake Snyder's beat system, Joseph Campbell's Hero's Journey, the popular 7-point story structure as explained by Dan Wells, and even Lester Dent's method (he used to churn out the Doc Savage series pulp fiction during the Depression) you'll see that they really all align with each other to describe the same basic method.

Whether a story is short or long, they contain the same basic story arcs.

What's different in a serial is that they have that structure *both* in short form for that episode, and in long form for the longer story arcs that the characters are moving through.

Your serial may have chapters in it. Each chapter has those five parts and contributes overall to the 3-Act format your serial is following. Or your serial may just be a short story or even flash fiction (a thousand words or less.)

However, your serials add up into a longer story arc.

The best examples we have these days are long-running TV series using "seasons" as a container to hold serial episodes of continuing stories. Each season has episodes which each may or may not have cliffhangers to get you to watch the next one. It will have each character changing some way or the other and evolving through the series. And the readers (viewers) identify with those characters and want to pick up that story where they left off the last week, or the last season.

So you have to write serials while keeping in mind the over-arching changes the characters are going through.

Interestingly, you'll see these popular shows actually finish off major plots and continue the character's own personal plots. On Stargate, they defeated the main enemy to then get a worse enemy, to ultimately defeat that enemy, only to replace it with an even worse enemy. About that time, the show was canceled and they had to wrap it up with four movies. (Yes they had that much plot material left around.) The longer-running "Gunsmoke" was similar that way, as was "Murder She Wrote".

Star Trek was able to milk several movies and alternate shows out of the original TV series. The character arcs just kept continuing, along with new characters. And there were spin-off story lines that often ran parallel to each other and had fan-favorite crossovers.

Star Wars isn't just a series of movies, but has also taken on alternate story lines through comic books. Of course both DC and Marvel comic book characters from the 50's who have had long runs in that format are now finding new lives in the movies. And others have made the transition to TV from print. Smallville was arguably the longest running serial-based show in that format, tracing Superboy's progress to Superman, with all the love interests and villains along the way.

All these tell long stories, all cut into parts.

The question is: what ties these together and keeps the readers/viewers coming back for more?

5 DECENT TIPS ON WRITING SERIAL FICTION

HAVE AN OVERALL PLAN.

You can go into great detail, but figuring where each installment ends and how they contribute to where you want your season or series to end up – all that will strengthen your narrative. Such an outline will keep you on track. Threads you set up early will pay off later. There's also the idea that you may want to do a sequel (or even five) so the more long-scale planning you do, the easier your writing will end up.

That said, don't take the soul out of your story by dissecting it into immense amount of detailed figure-out. There is more fun for the writer when they know where each story starts, with what setting and what characters, and then know where it has to end for the next story to begin. If it's fun to write, it will be fun to read. Boring makes more boring.

Take Your Time.

You don't have to wrap up every plot nicely with a bow at the end of a story unit. Having the villain escape can be a nice touch your fans will enjoy (because they know that ultimate justice will be that much greater.) Often a minor sub-plot can turn into your main story line. Realize that your fans will be here for the long haul, so you'll want to string your story along and make it truly an experience.

But don't leave things hanging on forever.

Every story unit should go somewhere definite and enable certain changes for your characters to grow or evolve. The main plot for that episode or chapter should be definite on it's own. The exception would be a part one-part two scene where the audience is included in a longer story arc that can't be told adequately in just a single episode. And you can wrap up threads in a later story that are begun earlier. Plan your work, work your plan, keep your audience involved.

Give your supporting characters the occasional spotlight.

You can create a break in the action by having a minor character take the starring role for that episode. You'll be able to look at things through his viewpoint for awhile as he solves things while your main roles take a break (or are off doing things elsewhere.) But also make sure that it somehow advances the main story arc. One great part is that now your audience has someone else to root for.

What is easier done in written stories than TV series is being able to write from different character viewpoints. Romance is usually done this way – where you move from alternating character's minds as you work through the story.

Sneak in some fan rewards.

Your long-devoted fans will appreciate having some little inside jokes or obscure references to earlier episodes. Perhaps this is a way to move that little thread along and get it ready for the spotlight a few episodes from now. The truly devoted fans will catch this and be delighted with the nuance of meaning. Also, they'll be able to have something else to discuss in the forums. Hidden meanings can abound, but we really want to make it obvious delight. Keep it simple, though. Crack a joke or make the reference and then back to work on that episode's story arc.

You'll see this in long running TV series, where they play clips from earlier episodes that remind the audience what happened before this – and also then give a preview of what's going to happen in this next episode. All in about a minute or less at the beginning. Something that's almost impossible to pull off gracefully in writing text.

Sidebar: in my longer-running fiction series, I've had to refer to earlier books in the end pages, so that newer readers could know what to pick up to understand that minor character's backstory – where they were a main character. That also helped with the crossovers. After all, you have only so many words to spend in a short story episode...

5 MISTAKES TO AVOID WHEN CREATING SERIAL FICTION

YOU CAN FIND TRULY stupid advice anywhere on anything. The worst is from free downloads or friends and neighbors.

It was the same with this book. As I mentioned, this book was started out of necessity as the only two books on Amazon about serials were truly awful ripoffs. Oh, they had all the smart editorial reviews in all the right places, but when you started reading they just fell apart. Reviews mean nothing if sales suck.

This also happens when you try to study serial fiction. Even the people who have "successfully written" in this format can "say the darnedest things" and not disclose that they have no audience and don't sell well at all. Or that they give all their serial fiction away for free and make their living at a day job, writing only on the weekends.

You also have to watch out for people who wrote serial fiction 8 years ago (and dropped that style of writing) or mention about programs that have been shelved, like Kindle Serials.

Research has to be done into underlying evergreen principles which were used in Dickens' time as well as by the most popular and long-running serials today.

Here's a set of mistakes I've found that recur in the research taken to get this guidebook together:

1. **Commit suicide by just jumping right into your serial fiction.**

Serials are built in the endings. Quality stories are established at the beginnings with good hooks, good characters, and good settings.

In serial fiction, it's said that the first three chapters (episodes) are the anchor of the story. These are, in the broader story arc, the first act where you set up the story. Use them to establish your characters as you build the world you inhabit. Leave clues, build threads, establish minor story arcs you can build on later. By the third chapter, your ardent fans will be creating the world for you. Give them hints so their imagination can run free. Then they'll tell their friends.

While you should at least create the first three episodes (chapters) before you publish anything, it might be a smart idea to roughly organize the entire first season of episodes (collection of stories) so you have everything laid out. This will help your writing go faster.

2. Over- and under-planning might wreck your serials.

While stream-of-consciousness has helped many authors (particularly the avant-garde authors like James Joyce and Virginia Woolf) to their own fame, what was hidden in these authors is that they built their stories based on their own lives. So they actually had a framework to follow. While short stories come out great by writing standalone stories (particularly flash fiction) a serial by definition follows one after the other, building on the preceding.

What holds serials and any story line together is the long and evolving character arcs, not particularly the episode arcs. You are really following these characters through their various personal changes and they become part of your extended family as you tune into them weekly.

Build your grand arch plot, your character story arcs, and lay out each episode's particular problem-solving situation broadly. Then you can go writing along in each individual episode. But its tricky to jump in with no structure from the beginning. You may very likely wind up eight episodes in with nowhere to take your dead characters.

Not that it can't be done. But you're going to have to trust your muse, trust your characters, and be willing to write driving in the dark with dim headlights. Can be done. Has been done. Up to you.

Plot your future in general terms and then flesh out the details the way that best fits you and your muse.

3. Hang together with your team, or hang separately.

Serial writing has been described as only for A-listers. Because the demands on your time are extreme and unending. So having a support team that will edit and proof and walk your dog (occasionally) and allow you to pour your soul into their bottomless ear (more frequently) are all facets of your life as a writer you must allow people to help you with. Build a rudimentary team, if it's only people you trust at Fiverr to continue creating great covers for you.

Unless you have an independent income, and are already an experienced writer, plus have your own editing and graphic skills – you are facing possible burnout. Get a team, or take your time getting through the learning curves of self-publishing.

As I sometimes joke: after the first hundred books, it get's easier.

4. Don't worry about the characters, they'll show when ready.

Yes we're back to the weird world of writing with headlights again. You have main characters, and supporting characters. These also have individuals in their lives which need fleshing out, if only slightly. All of these are part of the world you build and present to your reader/viewer. Stories and their muse-agents will present new characters as needed. Your job is to write them into existence as best you can, as they do appear.

Some people use tools like Scrivener to keep notes about these, or put them onto a spreadsheet. Motivations, habits, quirks, favorite foods and activities, hidden secrets, interconnections.

You may want to keep these noted when you do work up your characters of all types and degrees of separation. They will help you flesh out your threads and give excitement to your readers/viewers as you continue through your serial, its episodes, and its seasons.

Calibre is a great tool to collect your stories. And build an ad-hoc collection of them in order so that you can then search through that assembled text to find out what characters generally wore, what their hairstyles are, and also any details you'll need to be consistent through the stories. Again, this is what your fans will notice and expect. You have to respect the world your devoted readers create from your details.

5. Read and write what you love – those are the best teachers.

Got your copy of Strunk's "Elements of Style"? That's great for non-fiction, not so useful for fiction.

There are rules to this craft which those English teachers tortured you into forgetting. Go ahead and keep them forgotten.

The best advice from both Stephen King and Dorothea Brande is to learn by reading others' books. Dissect these, note where you put their books down, note which stories left you wanting more from that author. Figure out how they build their stories and why they had that effect on you. Then use those elements and strategies in your own writing.

Follow only professional authors who make a living at fiction writing instead of their day job. There are people who make their living as a university professor who write new books annually about the craft of writing. Mostly, these books are unmemorable. If you study any craft books, look up well-known authors who incidentally wrote a book about how they did it.

Most of your own writing will be by writing – lots. Lots.

A SHORT SURVIVAL GUIDE TO SHORT STORIES

YOUR SURVIVAL AS A writer is at stake.

You need to listen to this, because there are rules and there are Rules.

We've covered how and if plotting is done, and when you let your muse dictate to you.

Next is the real mind-creaking internal journey all authors must confront and slay, or run screaming and crying into the night:

Short stories have no real set length.

They follow the rules of story structure, but not always obviously.

Sometimes short stories have no room to be obvious.

But the basics are always there, even for a minor character making a cameo appearance.

And this probably isn't the place to describe all that a short story is and isn't. But it does deserve a mention.

It deserves its cameo.

The bottom line to success in any story is to appeal to the archetypes we are programmed with from birth, if not before. But everything doesn't fit into the Hero's Journey. So don't try. Stick to what is needed for the story – and will fit within 6,000 or 12,000 words.

As in flash fiction, some elements have to be implied.

Like world building. As Robert Heinlein is quoted, "The door dilated." Instant world.

OK, maybe not that simple.

But your story has always: Beginning, Middle, End.

Your character goes through both external and internal changes.

There are also always a Hook, Crisis, and a Payoff. (And for serials: a cliffhanger.)

Or you can run through the simpler "story shapes" as Vonnegut called them. (See his video and the study the University of Indiana did on these – links in the Appendix and endpages.) You'll still have changes in the character(s) of the story depending on the problem they are solving, and their own needs.

The point is that you have to master storytelling. And you can be as verbose as you want, or as miserly.

One approach is to pick your wordage, cut it into four parts, and then work from there. (The center two parts form the second act.) Now you have a few hundred or a few thousand or several thousand words to create the effect you need in each part.

Look up books on Short Stories and work out the basics for yourself. The more you know, the more you've tested for yourself, the more practice applying those basics, the better your work will be.

And, obviously, the easier your story will be to market and sell. With a little luck derived from common sense, you can live a very comfortable life as a result.

Your choice. As usual.

HOW DO YOU SELL THESE FRICKIN' THINGS?

I HAD TO DELETE AND rewrite this chapter after I'd been writing and selling fiction for a few years.

You're going to have to get over worrying about whether they are ever going to sell.

First, Amazon and most ebook outlets are super-saturated with all sorts of ebooks. And as I mentioned, longer works sell better. Particularly when they are published in print.

But you want to start by writing short stories and putting them up as ebooks for sale through online outlets.

Go ahead and do it. Then write your next one. And publish it that same week. Figuring that you want to get up to writing some 12K words per week. That's one or two stories you then publish. When you have about 150K words, then you can publish a collection, or edit the stories into one massive 300-page tome.

Meanwhile you've been putting everything you've got up there for sale. And hopefully selling these as you go. But don't expect miracles.

The one write-up I mentioned earlier about the five-book series producing six-figure income for an author – she did it buy selling a "box set" for .99 in an ad to the uber-readers on Bookbub. Those are the readers that will plow through about two of those 300-page novels in a week. So they'll then buy your following two books at full price. Because you involved them in your character's life-stories.

That is a summation of the one model I've found where the bally-hooed success has occurred.

Meaning – prepare to be writing for five years, week after week, consistently, until you have enough content to package up into several collections - all in a long series.

But you write these short stories all in serials so they keep your readers hooked all the way through. And you write in series (this is where Game of Throne, Shades of Gray, Twilight, Divergent all set examples).

Most ebooks are sold by advertising to rise above the also-rans. Ebooks that pay their way are each thick, each in series. Takes years of writing to get these produced.

Meanwhile, you can get your opt-ins at the end of each book so people can join your email list. Another thing that happens at the end of these books is an updated list of (linked) books you've already written.

Now that is where it gets interesting. Because instead of six books to show for three years of writing, you have one or two per week. At the end of writing short stories in serials and series, you now have a hundred-fifty individual short stories and might have another 60 collections – so readers find you have 210 books they can buy. Yes, do the math: three years, over 200 books.

Yes, you can. Been there, done that.

Some of those are going to sell somehow, without running any ads.

At the end of five years, you have the equivalent of six 300-page novels. All (hopefully) in a long series. Then you can use that "six-figure" ad buy scene above to hook your audience and make your payday.

By the way, chasing up the modern-day "success stories" found that those writers worked between five and ten years at their writing and publishing in order to become "overnight" successes. That has been done in shorter time, and several one-shot wonders have happened. Right place, right time, right prose style. But they couldn't duplicate it.

Learn your craft and hone your work habits. That's what writing and publishing every single week will accomplish. You'll become inured to these "get rich quick" guru's. They make their money selling non-fiction books and courses to wanna-be's.

Any small business has to be able to run three years without making a dime of profit. Figure that your fiction writing is a business. Set yourself up from the get-go with an independent income (or supportive, loving spouse) to cover your costs while you learn your craft. While you build your back list.

Persistence is what counts.

As Earl Nightingale pointed out, first you become successful by delivering exceptional value, only then does the money roll in.

BUILDING YOUR SERIALS FOR SUCCESSFUL SALES

WHILE YOU START WITH the end in mind, you also start well in order to end well.

How you structure the book and how well you write the individual episodes monitor how well you will sell. Again, it's quality books produced in volume.

We've heard the horror stories of failure. But we also note that the authors doing this are taking short-cuts and getting caught out.

If you're going to write longer novels, then do that.

But the people writing short stories who master the craft have no problems finding their books sell and continue to sell. Especially when selling their short stories as Kindle ShortReads, and then compiling them into collections and "boxed sets."

Now, let's get some terms straight for this project:

(We're using TV terms as these are easier for those of us raised on weekly dramas instead of Dickens' Pickwick Papers.)

An individual serial short story – episode.

A collection of 16 episodes – season.

A collection of 4 episodes - season part.

The general plan I see at this point is to publish a "season collection" as well as publishing quarters of the seasons as collections.

Episodes are probably 6,000 words, to be published as individual short stories.

Season parts are at about 24,000 words (4 episodes) and can be published through print on demand. (Yes, that's thin. Easy to slip into a purse or briefcase, even a wide pocket.)

The full season is 16 episodes, as that is pretty close to industry standards for TV series, and also works with the 3-Act structure (1st Act 4, 2nd Act 4+4, 3rd Act 4. Four episodes to a season-part collection) This can give you another paperback, and is thick enough to print your author name and book title on the spine, big enough for people to read.

Why 4 episodes as the minimum collection? It gets the series well underway with the characters and settings established, as well as the longer story arcs. Each part-season collection then follows the next Act.

With me so far?

So that means you are cranking out a season every 8 to 16 weeks.

By the end of a year's worth of work (technically, 48 weeks) you might have have 6 seasons created. Each of these are in their own collection and paperback. That's 48+12+3=63 books published and on-sale. About 290K words per year, or just over 1100 pages at 250 words per page (the standard for ebooks). In print (at 300 words per page) that's about 960 pages. Over three big novels in length.

That may seem unreal – but you aren't having to shoot the movie every week. What's unusual for most is the simple math of how simple ebook and Print on Demand paperbacks can be produced. We are still producing (only) two or three 300-page novels a year. And now you know how simple that can be. Just working in the small parts rather than huge page-counts and all that entails.

All you're doing is writing and publishing a 6,000 word short story every week. Simple in theory, a little more difficult in practice. Has been done by many before you.

Meaning that in one year, you've just created a publishing empire and given your fans something to look forward to when they discover one of your books and love it.

Pricing

Follow or ignore the conventional wisdom at this point. Amanda Hocking made her claim to fame by selling several big novels in a few series at .99 each. Those days are gone – because Amazon changed their algorithm. She became an "overnight" millionaire after writing for some five years, having 10 full novels under her belt and ready to sell.

Sell your short stories for what they are worth, and then the collections will be more of a value.

Delivery

Instead of publishing to each of the five main book outlets, you might consider publishing through an aggregator like Draft2Digital. Pay them 10% for saving you time that you should be writing.

This is all straight-ahead writing. Into the dark with headlights on. Trusting your muse. No drafts, some revisions after proofing. Publishing the same week as you finish writing.

And Audiobooks...

If you use reading aloud to do your proofing, you may consider editing those saved recordings into audiobooks. That takes another chunk of time. But if you're as expressive with your voice as you are through your typing fingers, then it can also be an additional revenue stream.

You can also then giveaway MP3 recordings as a bonus to new readers and old. Podcasts off dramatic readings are welcome – and they sell the ebook, paperback, and audio versions of the book.

The point is to immerse your audience in these episodes and start expecting to see what is happening with their favorite characters as the series continues.

But that's a lot of plates spinning all at once, a lot of balls in the air.

Most people can't.

You've been warned.

HOW TO STUDY SUCCESSFUL TV SERIALS TO WRITE BETTER

OF COURSE, I FOUND this out from someone else. But writers have been studying/copying/stealing from other authors forever.

As early as Ray Bradbury, writers have been using movies as an alternative to reading others books. You can consider a movie to be a novella or novelette, at one minute per page of text. (1:30 is 90 pages, is 23K words.)

TV shows generally are about 45 or 48 minutes. (Meaning 12K words – a short story.)

This is also how the 3 Act story structure works.

- Act 1 - first 12 minutes.

- Act 2a - second 12 minutes.

- Act 2b - third 12 minutes.

- Act 3 - final 12 minutes.

You'll also see from where we covered story structures, that most follow this break down. If you check Lester Dent's formula for how he treats his hero in the Doc Savage pulps, you'll see that it's all in four sections, getting far more intense every time. And Dent was writing for a 6K-word story in that write-up.

This also predicts your page count. Starting from an 8,000 word goal, each of those sections is 2,000 words long. And if you write it so that there is a break in the action just before a commercial, then it will seem normal to you.

Now to save you time, so you don't have to re-watch these episodes, you can look them up on IMDb for full plot treatments. This would also be a good time to study through the overall character arcs for the series, season by season. That will be good homework to build an over all story arc as well as maintaining the individual character arcs.

However, I've found that buying the complete series is a better way of studying long episodes. As well, the acting will give you visual clues on how to write the sequences for maximal emotional impact.

Yes, this is a lot of work.

Yes, I told you this isn't a walk in the park.

But do you want to work smart or just work hard?

PART THREE - ARE SERIALS SOMETHING TO BUILD AT HOME?

THE RISE AND FAILURE OF POPULAR SERIALS

NOW WE'VE FOUND HOW writing profitable serials is all but impossible.

The worst model you can use is trying to compare yourself to Charles Dickens. In those days, books were very expensive and the populace mostly illiterate. The inexpensive periodicals which published serials in those days actually were teaching people to read and appreciate stories. There was no competition from TV or radio or movies or streaming on-demand video.

The stories you are writing now have to grab a reader's interest and suck them into the vortex of action before they know what hit them.

What you won't be doing is to study the form and language of long-dead authors in order to impress our current generations with classic style and grammar. They won't buy it.

What you will need to do is to master your own work-ethic and talent to find new and exciting ways to stand out among the wannabes and also-rans.

Your secret weapon, once again, is to study the most popular serials of all time - which are TV series which have run multiple years. Most of these have had different directors, different producers, and the casts have changed out. ("Stargate" killed off one of its main characters several times over the years, only to revive him again and again.)

The story is what lived. The screenwriters would change, but the story had a life of its own. Until it finally ran its course – or not.

Yes, lousy writing, dumb producer decisions, and stupid acting has killed TV serials. If a written serial isn't popular, it is the fault of the writer alone. (While there are also stupid network decisions, such as the premature burial of "Firefly" and scheduling the original Star Trek TV series for late at night.)

There is life in any story, says Chris Vogler in his "Writer's Journey." By his Third Edition, he'd added an essay in the appendix titled "Stories Are Alive" where he traces how stories continue to have lives of their own after they make their original birth into our culture. They can reborn, reworked, recast, refilmed, rewritten. The story can change or it can stay the same. But it's alive and out there.

So don't think your serial is dead because no one loves it. Even if you only wrote it to get it out of your system so that your muse would let you sleep at night. Perhaps it is an evil monster. But even monsters have a theme, have a mission, have a reason for existing.

As you write a serial, it simply has to appeal to the archetype-shorthand that we all use to understand the world around us. Vogler's book is an excellent introduction to that shorthand, better even than Joseph Campbell's original academic tome. Because Vogler wrote *as* a writer *for* writers.

You are the midwife, the go-between for the story you bring to life.

You can always go back and make it better, re-title it, get new covers made, get new reviews, republish it on different platforms, lower the price, raise the price... You can do anything and everything you can to breathe life into it and give it wings to find its own way in the world.

It won't be for want of trying.

The better your skill (which comes with study and practice) the easier this will become for later stories.

And there is even another option: several artists and writers actually only ever paint or write the same story over and over and over. People buy these and never get tired of them.

Because people want symbols and stories in their lives to help them make sense of everything. They want to reach the point where their emotional needs and rational wants match. At that point they buy. At that point, they have something that helps them "make sense" out of this sometimes chaotic and confusing world.

You then have a hit on your hands.

And meanwhile, you've already started working on the next one.

ARE SERIALS SIMPLY IMPOSSIBLE TO WRITE, MARKET, AND PROFIT?

IT JUST MIGHT BE THAT you've read this far only to see that writing serials isn't for you.

Serials are hard to write, probably harder than novels. Certainly harder than non-fiction.

But if you think about it, don't all chapters in a book somewhat follow the pattern of a serial?

The trick is that they aren't written to fit the dual duty of both standalone episode and mortar between two bricks in the wall. Good serials are. Novels split up into pieces don't.

And this is probably what you are running up against.

Serials are hard to write. There are no shortcuts.

Serials make different demands on your time. They are a marathon, not a sprint. Standalone short stories are a foot race. One and done. Serials have mile after mile after mile. And on the Boston Marathon, there is a section known as Heartbreak Hill, where the steady upward climb has killed more hopes of potential winners than any other section. (Not too oddly, that matches the part of the Three Acts as a Crisis.)

But for the real writer, the world can now be understood as a Serial. You have seasons of episodes and your journey continues, or a new one starts.

As you study and practice, your writing should become easier.

There is an old story of a person passed over for promotion. When he asked why this other person (who had been at the firm less time than he had) was more qualified, he was told that he had more experience.

He then retorted, "But I've had more years at the job."

And was told, "And you've done the same job for all that time, over and over. You relived the same experience during that time. The other guy sought out different experiences and learned more tools and solutions he could use to solve more problems for the company. That's why he got the job."

The shortcutter doesn't make it at anything until they realize they need to learn and apply the basics.

It doesn't help in our world that some shortcutters can make millions "over night." What you don't see is where they eventually lose it all, or the miserable lives (of the rich) they lead because they try to short-cut everything in their lives. You only see their brief moment in the sun.

There are rules and there are Rules. There are the law of human societies and there are Universal Laws. Some can be bent or broken without consequence, if there is no one to enforce them. The others are policed by greater forces than you can imagine. And those stories are told through the ages.

<u>The moral</u>: Short cut and fail. Study, learn, know your crafts of writing and marketing. Then you succeed to the degree you have faith in yourself and apply what you learn. And you persist on your own journey.

AND JUST WHEN YOU FELT LIKE GIVING UP...

THE DARKEST PARTS ARE just before the dawn.

And any writer can "hit the wall" occasionally on any project.

I've tried here to tell you some ideas you can use to avoid this problem. For it isn't a cliché - it's very real.

Implied or implicit, it's in every story you write. It's an archetypal situation that is met by any hero(ine) on any journey.

And yet, you know you just can't do this stuff. You've tried and failed, and tried again and failed again.

Maybe thousands of times, like Edison and his light bulb experiments. Or the 39 times before WD-40 was perfected.

I'm here to tell you now: *persist.*

Eventually, you'll have a breakthrough. The clouds will part (if only slightly) and the world will get a bit more rosy as everything starts to work out.

Yes, serials can be hard. They can be impossible to write. And you can wind up facing a plot hole that condemns your project to a screeching or quiet halt.

Do you then re-write?

Do you then go back to the editor and beg for help?

Do you shelve the project and maybe never pick it up again for years or ever?

This is what faces you now.

Maybe you took a shortcut. Time to go back and un-do that.

Maybe you freewrote when you should have planned. Time to go back and do that, then come forward from there.

Maybe you do need to do some massive re-writes. (Sigh.)

What do you do?

Whatever you decide, it's between you and your muse and your audience.

If you are truly willing to "kill your darling" then you can yet have success with this.

No, eating crow doesn't taste good regardless of the seasoning. Pride goes before a fall, but the only problem with falling is when you don't get back up (as Mary Pickford used to say.)

PART FOUR – ONE SERIAL TO RULE THEM ALL

HOW YOU COULD WRITE YOUR OWN SERIAL SUCCESS STORY

IF YOU'RE READING THIS, you have courage beyond most writers. You weren't scared off by all the warnings, trolls, and great gray whales.

It's not impossible to write successful serials.

It does take planning, and nothing succeeds without your putting your best into it. That means work.

0. Setup

Schedule your day so you spend your most inspired time writing, and an equal amount of time marketing.

Ensure you aren't interrupted while you are supposed to be writing.

Set daily word goals and make them.

Read books in your genre any spare moments otherwise.

1. Book Structure

Set up a spreadsheet that grids out what happens when. You'll probably need one for the series.

And maybe one master sheet for you character arcs. But don't overdo it. Let your characters come to life as you write.

Figure out how much writing you can get done in a day's worth of work. If you only have an hour per day to write, then see what your best can be – which is publishable words, not just a speed-typing test.

I've kinda settled on the 8-story series. This is 2 stories for each of the 3-Act parts, and so it easier to work out what tension and what action needs to be where. Even though each story has to stand on it's own, the pacing of a story in the last half of the 2nd Act will be faster and more intense than either the beginning or end ending stories. Just the way people expect it.

2. For each episode:

Consult the story just before it and where it needs to end.

Then crank it out, one episode at a time. If you've got the whole day, write your 6K words at one go.

The next day: proof it, revise it, tweak it, publish it.

Here's a tip from the TV series: At the end of an episode, there is a little bit tacked on that leaves the audience hanging – and wondering what that was all about, or how that is going to affect things. Meaning – you pick up resolving the cliffhanger (partially) that you left in the earlier book. Then you write your 6K-word story. Once you've got everything settled, then include a short part after that which is a cliffhanger for the next story.

I haven't written about cliffhangers in this story, but the general rule is that it's an incomplete character change or action-sequence. Something drastic is about to happen, either way.

Meaning: pick up where the earlier book left off, keep writing to the end where it's supposed to, then start writing the next book's action – but quit abruptly.

3. Publish on schedule every week. Once you have four or eight stories, compile them into a collection and publish that. (Editing is simple, since they are all already proofed and published.)

Set your episodes to come out weekly until complete.

4. Once your books are thick enough (about 64 pages) print the paperbacks. That probably means at every collection. Eight 6K stories will be 48K words, or close to 200 pages. It's just a few more minutes to create the paperback version through D2D once you have the ebook version published.

5. Then start your next story.

———

THIS IS JUST THE BROAD strokes, but gives you an idea of what's ahead of you.

Book publishing and marketing are covered in many other good books, and are quite beyond the scope of this simple edition.

See the endpages for other links and resources.

Your success is, and always has been, completely up to you.

THE NEEDS AND WANTS OF THE SERIAL WRITER

YOU'VE SEEN THIS IN your story structure studies: every character in your story has a need and a want.

The want is the object they are chasing, their goal, and for the antagonist, Hitchcock's "MacGuffin."

The need is internal, the unmet emotion or feeling the character is lacking. Whether they know it or not.

Separately, I've written about the five physical story structures that form all plots and genres. Writing is too simple once you master these and other basics.

You as the author, want to understand how to write serials and earn extra income (or make a living) doing this.

You as the author may need many things that success in this field will give you. For some, it's the relief of your muse leaving you alone for awhile (until that next inspiration strikes.) For others, it's the cathartic relief of having the story take on it's own life, as you've written parts of yourself into it. Now you can let your emotional past go. Adieu. Goodbye.

Some people can pursue the gossamer goal of public adoration and approval.

A piece of advice here: define these things for yourself.

At this point of this short book, you have all the tools you need to write successful serials – forever. What is left is for you to internalize your craft and practice until they become second nature.

Like any performance art, there are only so many bad performances in you. But enticing the good and excellent ones out depends on learning from your mistakes and seeing honest reviews of your craft.

Then your wants and needs can all be fulfilled.

At that point, pick out some new goal and get going on your next journey.

THE SERIAL WRITER RODE OFF INTO THE SUNSET, SINGING...

AT LEAST THAT'S HOW the old western serials used to go. Tex Ritter, the Lone Ranger, Gene Autry, Roy Rogers, and all those cowpokes. (And how about Annie Oakley?)

The darkest hours are behind you - for now.

You may yet face the most powerful antagonist ever. But that episode is around the corner, not today.

Hidden in this book are some strategies and tactics which can make your serial-writing easier and more profitable. As well, you'll need to do additional hours of study on related books and materials. I've left you plenty of links to follow within this book and in the end pages.

I am on my own journey to improve my own writing, publishing, and marketing. The life we both seek, apparently, is greater ease at doing what we most love.

For both of us, this stage of the journey is nearly complete.

So I wish both of us the best of luck.

PART FIVE – APPENDIX

THE ART OF WRITING CLIFFHANGERS

Lists of Cliffhanger Types

A CLIFFHANGER IS NAMED after the trope of having the chapter end up with the hero hanging off a cliff, literally. And the next chapter says how he solves it. So you read on.

But otherwise, I've assembled these notes:

At Writing.com, several examples of the various types of cliffhangers are taken from popular books.

A cliffhanger is when the writer ends a chapter or scene at a tense moment to encourage the reader to continue on to the next chapter.

In the 1800s, "penny dreadful" books became popular—and so did cliffhangers. Published in weekly parts, the books were cheap and exciting and often ended in the middle of a thrilling scene to encourage people to buy the next week's installment.

This site names 6 types of cliffhangers:

Character in Physical Danger

This is probably the most successful type of cliff-hanger. If you put the character in immediate danger, the reader will almost always read on.

Character Heading Into Danger or Mystery

When the characters are going into a dangerous place or possibly into a risky situation.

Surprise Reveal

An important piece of information, a person. or anything that shows up unexpectedly.

Emotional Tension

Emotional tension comes when there's a conflict between characters.

The Announcement of a Daring Plan or a Decision About Future Action

This type of cliffhanger revs up the story and the reader's interest because it promises that something new and exciting will happen very soon.

Something Bizarre or Confusing or Out of Character

A puzzling occurrence or comment that surprises both the characters and the readers and seems to have no explanation.

Karen Woodward has her own list pulled (via Anne M. Leone) from "Plot & Structure" by James Scott Bell (who called them "read-on prompts"):

- Impending disaster

- Dangerous emotions

- Portent

- Mysterious dialogue

- Secret revealed

- Major decision / vow

- Announcement of a shattering event

- Reversal / surprise

- Question left in the air

In Leone's article, she reviewed her favorite books for examples.

D. W. Smith has one or more courses built around cliffhangers and endings. Again, he mainly just tells lists of types.

To learn cliffhangers, work out carefully how every chapter in your favorite stories end. You read and dissect to improve your endings and make them hook the reader into the next. Chapter endings have the cliffhangers, and these are different from book endings. (And give you a clue to writing short stories as serials.) They have to fit within the reality of that story you have your hands on. They have to meet reader expectations. Or that reader will put down your book for no known reason for them, and won't probably pick up another book by that pen name.

(Which is again why you should practice and publish under multiple pen names across various genres.)

The other approach is to watch the long-running serials and see how they do it. Most of this is figuring out how the characters are going to resolve an over-arcing problem. And you have the character arcs versus the individual story arcs and the longer-running arcs. The 10-year (and 3 spin-offs, plus three movies) run of Star Gate can tell you a lot of how cliffhangers work. There are other series, in full-feature films that also do this. Die Hard is one. Another is the Dark Knight trilogy with Christian Bales. Of course, the original first three Star Wars movies and of course Star Trek (I prefer the three alternative-history movies with Chris Pine.)

Remember, half-hour shows are the equivalent of short stories, full hour shows are novellas, and multi-part hour shows or feature-length movies get close to novel length (corporate published novels, that is.) That's why the biggest classics have to be abridged to make it into film, because a 100-page romance would have to be told over five movies, maybe three if they were feature length. And the stories aren't written like that. Dickens stories, the ones he serialized, would be the exceptions. Keep that in mind as you study these stories and their movie counterparts..

Basics to Cliffhangers

THERE ARE CERTAIN BASICS that you are going to need to know in order to understand (and dissect) cliffhangers:

- Aldis Budrys Plot Skeleton

- Lester Dent Story Formula

- Plotto Theme Elements

- The Three Physical Plot Structures

- Vonnegut's Story Shapes

Now, we are going to add one more: **Orson Scott Card's MICE.**

In his "Characters & Viewpoints" Card figures that stories build emphasizing a central factor. It isn't all just plot, it isn't all just characters. As Card says:

The four factors are milieu, idea, character, and event.

> - *The **milieu** is the world surrounding the characters — the landscape, the interior spaces, the surrounding cultures the characters emerge from and react to; everything from weather to traffic laws.*

> - *The **idea** is the information that the reader is meant to discover or learn during the process of the story.*

> - ***Character** is the nature of one or more of the people in the story — what they do and why they do it. It usually leads to or arises from a conclusion about human nature in general.*

- *The **events** of the story are everything that happens and why.*

He goes on to say that some stories are heavy on world building (science fiction and fantasy), idea (fables, children's stories, mystery-detective), character (most romances), events (action-adventure, thrillers.) This doesn't say you can't have cross-genre/sub-genre mash-ups – a romantic fantasy would be one example.

The point here is that depending on what your book leans heavily on, you can use the basic definition of cliffhanger to construct them through world building or idea in addition to the most common cliffhangers that have to do with events or character emotion.

Macbeth's Three Witches Still Haunt Every Story

PROBABLY THE BEST HOOK I've seen was Shakespeare's Macbeth. That scene of three witches set the entire play up. The next scene was seeing a ghost. Great stuff. A tragic murder mystery. That starts with a cliffhanger.

In every story you have to introduce three elements in the first act, just as fast and deeply as you can:

- Character

- Setting

- Problem

That's the first step of Budrys Framework. Most people refer to "conflict" when they are talking about plotting, but it's a limited term. Go back to William Wallace Cook's Plotto and you'll see the principle point the character is trying to resolve is "a goal opposed." And that is one of the definitions of problem. It's also describes conflict.

Through any story, the characters have emotional changes as they learn and adapt (or tragically fail.) Settings will change as background and as the result of actions. The problems can (and usually do) get worse before they resolve.

Within this, you can have multiple characters that wind up changing by interacting with each other.

Once you set up these three elements above, then your character(s) set out to attempt to solve their problem(s). (See Budrys' format again.) These are called try/fail cycles. Our most popular fiction has these in sets of three: try/fail, try/fail, try/succeed.

In each of these cycles you have character reaction to what just happened. So the formula becomes try| fail/succeed | react.

Interrupting any of these can be a cliffhanger.

The places where you interrupt is at the high or low points of their story shape. Vonnegut was mainly talking about emotional highs and lows that a character goes through in a story. The cliffhanger interrupts the story right at the peak or the valley in that story.

Every story has four parts, as laid out by the Lester Dent Formula. (You split the second act in two, basically.) At each of these splits, you're supposed to have a plot-shift or plot-twist.

All through the story, in our modern Western plots, the tension is building as everything goes along. Lester Dent describes this well. But you also need to take into account the story shapes. Based on Vonnegut's story shapes, scientists ass the Computational Story Laboratory did a study of the emotional content of our most popular stories. They determined that three shapes were most popular, in a set sequence:

> *In particular, the team says the most popular are stories involving two sequential man-in-hole arcs and a Cinderella arc followed by a tragedy.*

Chart out the emotional content of your story, then interrupt a peak or valley while building suspense in the reader.

If you again look at those lists of cliffhangers, you can find that they have a single principle in common:

> *"Interrupting the change of character/setting/problem with built-in suspense."*

Or, more simply:

"Expected resolution disrupted."

And that means that you aren't ending things where they should. You're purposely ending them with a teaser that is completed or answered in a later (not necessarily the next) chapter or episode. It's the suspense that keeps you turning the page to find out what happens next or how it turned out.

Readers have to turn the page to find out what happens next.

The craft is in how to build them into your story. (If you said to never finish your chapter, you're on the right track...)

Writing Stories From The Ends Toward the Middles

THIS SINGLE CLIFFHANGER principle starts laying out how and where to write your stories. You want to quit ending things where they are expected. Instead of Start-Middle-End, you're going to have your resolution end somewhere in the early part or middle of your chapter, along with some breathing space, and then you start ramping it up (or down) again and again leave the reader hanging.

This doesn't make logical sense – because this is a game of involving the readers feelings and emotions, not their abstract thinking. But once you get the habit of interrupting them when they least want or need, then you'll have it.

You could even take up stories of your own that you've abandoned for some reason (usually because they became too boring or predictable) and then study them again to add or subtract and split at the real stress-filled points. Publish and then write some more.

This probably means a study of books that were successfully serialized and are still selling/downloaded today.

Louis L'Amour is famous for never going out of print, and so are Lester Dent's "Doc Savage" stories. Mostly, the best stories involve you intrinsically one way or another – so the ones that keep you riveted are the ones you need to dissect. The ones you drop are the ones you can forget about.

Again, cliffhangers just involve mainly cutting right before everything finishes. But then you have to start again. So the endings and beginnings have to match.

Now, there are shifts, particularly when you're telling the story from more than one viewpoint. So you could leave the hero in peril, and then go back to the ranch where the heroine is in her own difficulty. That's a setting shift as well – so make sure you remind your reader with tags from when you've been there before – or give the reader a thorough grounding so they are sucked right into the story again.

W. D. Smith brought up another point, where the hero simply blacks out. (Knocked unconscious, etc.) And he tells of a story where a guy wakes up 7 years later as he's been in a coma the entire time. So there can be time shifts as well. Again, you'll have to bring the reader up to speed.

The straight-ahead Lester Dent story would leave the hero in a jam and then pick up the next section or chapter by getting the hero out of that jam. One point of caution here is that you can't assume your reader didn't put the book down. So your opening has to be the best of both worlds. You see this on TV where there are "Earlier on [TV Series Name]..." clips from whatever tells the viewer that is coming up referenced in earlier episodes.

TV series, particularly told over several seasons, are currently some of the best current examples of cliffhangers. Not only do they cut it so you will return after a commercial break, but so you will be waiting pensively for the series to start up again in their next season.

But Wait... The Larger Story is Like the Episode

THE FORMAT OF EACH cliffhanger is similar to the overall story. In serials, you have a hook, the episode itself and a teaser at the end. Hook is sunk to get them into the story. Teaser is to get them into the next installment. A lot of TV shows work the teaser in as 3-5 minutes of new action just before the credits. The last part then will either leave you with an action incomplete, or spend a little time on a minor arc, like the unfulfilled love interest.

An excerpt from an upcoming book is often used this way, although most are clumsy and disjointed, unless they continue the series.

A practice work, especially a long story or novel that is giving you problems, would be to break that story up into serials. Take the chapter breaks out. Now split the book right in the middle of an action, emotional, or scene shift. Each type of resolution is left incomplete somehow. Then you'll start seeing if it can be improved with a cliffhanger.

Don't forget that a resolved scene for a main character might leave a minor character unfulfilled. Such as two main characters in a surprise warm embrace, while a third character arrives with flowers and a box of chocolate. Mouth opens and eyebrows signal disappointment...

Lots to work with here.

If you don't have one of your own, you can always re-write a classic from a long dead author, or do a mash-up between two stories.

Best is simply to write a new story and look for inventive ways to keep it moving for the reader.

One point is to never let your book become predictable. If the reader knows you're going to leave them hanging, they may resent it. So you can change around your types of cliffhangers until you are able to use any of them easily. And do so.

This is a different way of looking at writing, and looking at life.

Now you'll see and write your stories from the inspiring world around you with new interest and new possibilities. And if you do, your readers will. So they'll come back for your next book and the one after that...

A Cliffhanger Side Bar

I MENTIONED BEING ON the butt-end of a disappointing six-week auto-workshop from D.W. Smith. The videos had been recorded years before. But he promised that he had actually studied cliffhangers and was going to lay it all out.

As I covered before, he only gave lists of lists.

And resolved for me that the real cliffhanger ran on interrupting major changes in action, character, or setting. Too simple to state, and takes a lot of practice to perfect. (The funny part is that he laid out covering The Seven Types of Cliffhangers, and then said what he'd cover in the next video – which you then had to wait a week for. So there can be cliff-hangers in non-fiction, too.)

My solution was to buy his course, then put off starting it until six-weeks later. That way I could go straight through. And meanwhile, my attention wasn't tied up in waiting. And yes, I resented having a six-week delivery time. So I kept busy researching other's lists and examples.

Finally through his cliffhanger course, I found Smith missed discovering that real underlying principle – as he's a genre-fiction author. He isn't a researcher who looks for systems of principles. He works on churning out the next story from boilerplate plots, elements, characters.

By the time I finished his course, I found no one else had worked this out, either. They knew how to write cliffhangers, but had no simple definition for them other than lists. Now you do.

One thing nagged at me, though. Smith mentioned a "theme cliffhanger" but then failed to describe it except in a few minutes of one video at the last week. Just tossed it off. Essentially, it consisted of *interrupting the reader's expectations for that specific genre.* That really goes back to one of those three interruptions above, but would be genre-specific. Mystery-detective would be simple here. Like the sudden realization that the trail was a red herring specifically left by the antagonist/villain – right at the end of a chapter.

What you've actually got is a combination of a couple of elements at the same time, usually a pairing of action and character reaction. Those are more common as you look for them. The harder version is getting setting in there as well, which is probably a scene shift at the beginning of the next chapter (right at the point Holmes concludes his only action is to take Moriarty over Rickenback Falls – the next scene is now back in their 221b flat in London where Watson is writing it all up, weeks later.)

If there is any sort of thematic cliffhanger, it would be where multiple combinations of the three elements are interrupted in the same scene ending. What would probably be more like this was to have a single scene (or several in sequence) where the three most common structural plots (action-adventure, romantic, mystery) all cross over close together or simultaneously. Typically, this is the crisis around the third act, just before the last set of commercials.

Meaning that there are four, five, or six cliffhangers to each TV production, depending on your script and shooting structure. But those are all short stories, including movies (which might rise to the length of a novella.) Novels can have cliffhangers at the end of each chapter and have a hundred chapters or more. Just those few principles gives you tons of study and practice to do. (You're welcome.)

HOW TO IMPROVE YOUR SPEED AND QUALITY AS AN AUTHOR BY WRITING LESS THAN MORE...

One Size Doesn't Fit All

ROBERT A. HEINLEIN (yes, that classic pulp fiction writer known for "Stranger in a Strange Land" and others) was wrong. But he was right at the same time.

He authored an essay, first published in 1947, titled "On the Writing of Speculative Fiction". It's been republished often and is available in many formats across the Internet.

The last section of this essay seems an after-thought. Yet this is where people only quote (partially) that last section and nit-pick it to death.

Here's what he wrote:

> *I'm told that these articles are supposed to be some use to the reader. I have a guilty feeling that all of the above may have been more for my amusement than for your edification. Therefore I shall chuck in as a bonus a group of practical, tested rules which, if followed meticulously, will prove rewarding to any writer. I shall assume that you can type, that you know the accepted commercial format or can be trusted to look it up and follow it, and that you always use new ribbons and clean type. Also, that you can spell and punctuate and can use grammar well enough to get by.*
>
> *These things are merely the word-carpenter's sharp tools. He must add to them these business habits:*

1. You must write.

2. You must finish what you start.

3. You must refrain from rewriting except to editorial order.

4. You must put it on the market.

5. You must keep it on the market until sold.

The above five rules really have more to do with how to write speculative fiction than anything said above them. But they are amazingly hard to follow–which is why there are so few professional writers and so many aspirants, and which is why I am not afraid to give away the racket! But, if you will follow them, it matters not how you write, you will find some editor somewhere, sometime, so unwary or so desperate for copy as to buy the worst old dog you, or I, or anybody else, can throw at him.

Heinlein was born in Butler, Missouri and grew up in Kansas City. He got an education at the U. S. Naval Academy in Annapolis, and after discharge, along with trying other work, he turned to writing. He published his first work in 1939. WWII interrupted this after 1942, but he returned to writing full time in 1945, next published in 1946.

His first full novel was published in 1947 (same as that essay.) Before that, he was writing short stories and short works which were quite popular. Very popular. So, on only three years of writing experience, we now have these rules for running a writing business that even he says are hard to follow.

That is the core problem people who have left their comments online don't understand about this. In three years, he was at the top of his profession. Show me anyone of these critics have done the same. Thought so. "Those who can't do, criticize."

With this, you can see Heinlein had a unique view of things. Unlike other pulp fiction writers, he actually didn't grow up in the pulp fiction era. He started writing short science fiction, which wasn't even a genre until after the first World War. The pulp magazines were actually in a decline and being replaced by paperbacks when he restarted writing after WWII.

So this was an author who had stumbled onto his particular talent for writing. He wrote about real humans, not machines. Heinlein knew how to write about the main character as someone who evolved during the story, who "learned better." And that is where he differed from many of the Sci-Fi authors, where the plot defined the character, rather than the character defining how the problem is solved due to their own internal strengths and weaknesses. The phrase for a plot-defined character is "melodrama." (Which comes from the silent movie days where the accompanist provided the melody for the drama.)

Back to Heinlein's business rules

YES, HE WROTE IN A day where people it only paid to be prolific. A penny per word. Write lots or starve. But according to his Wikipedia bibliography, he was only a middling-prolific author, as many authors wrote more, and many (lots and lots) wrote much less.

The key point of discussion is where *he recommends only re-writing to editor's order*. Re-writing is not the same as revising or editing. It is, in fact, rewriting the story from scratch. A second draft or third (or more, for modern novelists.) One author, Tom Simon – at bondwine.com – researched and found that Heinlein did in fact re-write "Strangers in a Strange Land." Practically, he wrote the book several times, completely starting over when the story wasn't going the way he wanted. When he at last got the right approach, he went ahead and finished it (something to do with placing the setting on Mars.) And *then* had to cut his story to fit them to publishable length (*Strangers* ended up a hair over 160K words, which makes all but modern Romance tomes pale in comparison.)

Simon also took D.W. Smith to task on this. But he hasn't apparently taken what Smith says with any serious study. Smith "cycles" through his writing, editing/revising/polishing as he goes. And by the end, they are very clean of errors. Smith says this is only possible with our modern computers. Before this time, many pulp fiction writers typed, used a carbon between two sheets, keeping a copy of their story for records.

Simon tells that Heinlein had trouble keeping his own rules. And illustrates these with many examples. The problem presented is in focusing on the errors instead of the ideal.

Smith points out in his short book about Heinlein's Rules that with his own personal method of "cycling", he can keep Heinlein's rules. That is his solution, change the method of writing and achieve the ideal. Smith also points out that very often, he will write before where the story should start and write after it should end. Then go back and delete those extra hundreds of words.

The premise for this is to cut the unnecessary parts off, as Bedford-Jones told us above.

The point here is that every writer will have to develop their own styles and methods of writing. Smith is simply holding up an ideal so a person can align their efforts toward it.

The rest of Heinlein's points few people object to:

1) **Write.** (Writers write – that is what they are supposed to do.)

2) **Finish what you write.** (Don't leave a bunch of stuff around without endings and so on.

3) **Don't re-write.** (Work out a system for clean final copy.)

4) **Put it on the Market** and

5) **Keep it on the market.** (Both of which are entirely possible in these days of self-publishing and electronic books that never go out of print.

Revising – a New Model Inspired by Heinlein and Movies

SHORT STORIES ARE THE building blocks to novels. Below these are scenes and beats (shots). Bradbury said each of his paragraphs was a shot in a scene. Lakin in her "Shoot Your Novel" also held that a scene was composed of shots:

> *This type of realistic behavior is what you want to capture in your fiction writing, and the way to do it is by utilizing various camera angles—the difference being that you have a specific intention in doing so. Rather than show a random encounter with boring dialog and nothing all that interesting happening in the scene—which is what real life often is like—you have an objective in playing this scene out, that high point you are leading to, a moment of revelation or plot twist that is going to deliver with a punch when you reach it. And so every camera angle is used deliberately to give the most punch when needed.*

> *Television producers follow a basic rule that no shot should last more than thirty seconds, and no scene should last longer than three minutes. This is the 30-3 Rule. This is the basic idea of how shot sequences are made. You take one long scene and break it down into a variety of short shots.*

> *How does this translate to fiction? A scene can take much longer than three minutes to read, and sometimes it may cover a number of moments in time, some even separated by days and weeks. But if you break down your scenes and look at the segments that take place, you will find a natural rhythm that feels just right.*

Scenes should be mini novels, with a beginning, middle, and end. It doesn't work to place strict rules on scenes, for they should be as long as they need to be—whatever it takes to effectively reveal the bit of story-line intended while keeping the pacing and tension taut. However, I believe if you lay out your scenes intentionally with a series of camera shots, leaving out excessive narration and backstory, your scenes will "move" like a movie and will feel like concise, succinct movie scenes.

The trick with books that were made into movies is that they always leave out tons of stuff. Again – is what you're reading really necessary to tell the story?

Brevity, The Soul Of Wit, Is Also Excellent Training

WE HAVE THE AVERAGE novel chapter (scene) being 2400 words, and divided into 30 paragraphs. While your pacing will change paragraphs from short to long and longer, you can figure that the average of these will be about 80 words long. A few sentences.

The other half of this is that self-published authors no longer have to cut a story down to its essence in order to publish (particularly when Romances will run to 120,000 words or more.)

Simon tells of cutting instead of rewriting,

> *"Heinlein was an engineer, and surely knew the rule of thumb that used to be called the 'RCA Principle', but is nowadays known as 'designing to manufacture': First build the best product you know how; then see how many parts you can eliminate before it stops working to specification. It is that elimination of superfluous parts that distinguishes a superior design from a merely adequate one, not only in engineering, but in art and literature as well."*

Take your story and cut it down by half and then fit the whole story into a flash fiction of 1000 or even 500 words. Just to see if it can be done. Then you'll give yourself two sets of stories to put on sale. The point of this and the Larkin excerpt above, is to improve your text by self-editing and paring down to the exact point that nothing enters a story unless it either forwards the action or defines the character.

You'll find that the story can be pared down only so far before it ceases to be a story. H. Bedford Jones, himself a million-word-per-year writer, held that stories were interwoven based on the intrinsic value of each part. He referred to Edgar Allen Poe's writing:

"Poe held that a story had an excellent plot when none of its component parts could be removed without detriment to the whole structure.... let your story be so written that not a paragraph of it could be cut out without positive detriment to the whole yarn—and you needn't worry about whether it has plot or not."

Not that you should routinely write flash fiction and make a living at it (although you could.) More that this can make your own writing so tight that you can quickly improve pacing and depth as you write, with little revising, and no re-writing.

Run each of these short-short stories through ProWritingAid.com as a side check and get a further learning opportunity out of it.

After a month of this, your own efficiency will speed up, as well as your writing speed and publishing speed. And that means your income potential can increase exponentially.

Of course, that means you must write and publish, and keep it all available for sale.

AS SEEN ON TV - THE HISTORY OF SERIALS AS WE'VE WATCHED THEM

AS SEEN ON TV, JUST not on your bookshelf - or is it?

You and I have spent our time and money following "favorite" shows from one season to the next. Like me, you probably have collections on DVD so you can re-watch episodes whenever you feel like it.

Netflix has found that by releasing all of a year's episodes at once, they have helped fuel a fad called binge-watching. This is where an entire season's episodes is viewed over a weekend or during a week. Often binge-watching is organized as a favorite activity with friends, even family.

Wikipedia has "binge watching" as:

> "Binge-watching, also called binge-viewing or marathon-viewing, is the practice of watching television for a long time span, usually of a single television show. In a survey conducted by Netflix in February 2014, 73% of people define binge-watching as "watching between 2-6 episodes of the same TV show in one sitting." Binge-watching as an observed cultural phenomenon has become popular with the rise of online media services such as Netflix, Hulu, and Amazon Video with which the viewer can watch television shows and movies on-demand.

> "History: The idea of assembling several consecutive episodes of a television series in order and watching them in rapid succession originated with the marathon, in which the television stations themselves programmed several hours' worth of reruns of a single series. This practice began in

the 1980s and is still popular among subscription television outlets.

"The usage of the word "binge-watch" can be traced as far back as the late 1990s, when it was used by circles of television fandoms. It has consisted of watching several episodes of a particular show in a row via DVD sets. Prior to the introduction of the DVD format, it was commonplace to record multiple episodes, or even entire miniseries to videotape to watch later in a single viewing session. The word's usage was popularized with the advent of on-demand viewing and online streaming. In 2013, the word "exploded" into mainstream use when "Netflix started releasing episodes of its serial programming simultaneously. 61% of the Netflix survey participants said that they binge watch regularly."

Why do people binge watch?

They are involved in a serial, which is episodic storytelling. This type of story involves the viewer or reader in the story arcs of recurring characters as they are involved in various situations weekly.

Serials are the oldest form of publication.

Wikipedia has this traced to the 17th century, where the development of movable type made printing affordable to the common person. Books, however, were still expensive and out of the budget of most. Authors found they could write and publish parts of their works and reach a broad audience.

"During the late 19th century, those that were considered the best American writers first published their work in serial form and then only later in a completed volume format. As a piece in Scribner's Monthly explained in 1878, 'Now it is the second or third rate novelist who cannot get publication in a magazine, and is obliged to publish in a volume, and it is in the magazine that the best novelist always appears first.' Among the American writers that wrote in serial form were Henry James, Harriet Beecher Stowe and Herman Melville. A large part of the appeal for writers at the time was the broad audiences that serialization could reach, which would then grow their following for published works.

"One of the first significant American works to be released in serial format is Uncle Tom's Cabin, by Harriet Beecher Stowe, which was published over a 40-week period by The National Era, an abolitionist periodical, starting with the June 5, 1851 issue."

This practice continued as it was profitable for both publications and authors up into the late 20th century. At this time, the expansion of broadcast television took most of this market.

Soap Operas as Serials

The American soap opera Guiding Light started as a radio drama in January 1937 and subsequently transferred to television in June 1952. Guiding Light was heard or seen nearly every weekday since it began, until 2009 making it the longest story ever told in a broadcast medium.

In the name, "soap" refers to the soap and detergent commercials originally broadcast during the shows, which were aimed at women who were cleaning their houses at the time of listening or viewing, and "opera" refers to the melodramatic character of the shows, according to Kate Bowles (from Soap opera: 'No end of story, ever' in The Australian TV Book, pg. 118)

Originally these serial TV shows were broadcast as fifteen-minute installments each weekday in daytime slots. In 1956, As the World Turns and The Edge of Night, both produced by Procter & Gamble Productions, debuted as the first half-hour soap operas.

Again, each story followed the main characters as they dealt with life stories, frequently marital problems.

> *"Romance, secret relationships, extramarital affairs, and genuine love have been the basis for many soap opera story-lines. In U.S. daytime serials, the most popular soap opera characters, and the most popular story-lines, often involved a romance of the sort presented in paperback romance novels. Soap opera story-lines sometimes weave intricate, convoluted and sometimes confusing tales of characters who have affairs, meet mysterious strangers and fall in love, and who commit adultery, all of which keeps audiences hooked on the unfolding story twists." (Wikipedia)*

As housewives more frequently entered the workplace, daytime soap opera viewership declined, and popular prime-time versions emerged, such as Dallas, Beverly Hills 90210, Desperate Housewives, and Scandal.

Serials as TV and Movie Productions

The over-arcing story has presented problems for TV shows. While avid viewers insist on this format, gaining new viewers is more difficult due to having to "catch up" to what is going on. As video recorders and later DVD releases (as well as the rise of Netflix and online downloads) this has been seen as less of a problem, as they can simply get earlier episodes and entire seasons.

Getting access to DVD's and direct downloads has caused problems in TV ratings, as these are not accessed over TV and so are not counted. Without accurate ratings, selling advertising has become more difficult.

The format for "TV" serials came from the same success they found in print, overarching plots with episodic adventures or stories which were resolved that week, adding to the longer questions of what was happening with the characters to remain unsolved.

With the standard 12-minute breaks in hour-long TV shows (for commercial advertisements) cliffhangers were employed so that viewers had to return to see how the characters resolved that situation. Infrequently, these also ran at the end of an episode, to encourage the viewer to return for the next scheduled episode. At the season finale's, these were often used to hook the viewers with a cliffhanger that could only be resolved in the next season's installments.

A famous episode was "Who Shot J.R.?" on Dallas, where the main character took a bullet in the final minutes of that season's finale.

HOW THIS BOOK WAS WRITTEN

THIS BOOK IS DEFINITELY not a serial.

But it does show that a 1st draft doesn't have to take forever.

The first draft was just over 8200 words long.

It took me something less than 12 hours to get to that point. (Interrupted by having to get some hay bales in before it rained.) And that included doing the research.

The first revision polished it up to around 10K words and took the greater part of the next day.

By the end of that week, the book was published to all major book outlets. Cover, meta-data, everything.

Which proves the general idea of having 8K worth of serials ready in a week.

(Three years later, I revised it over a couple of days, adding another 8K words pulled from other texts, just to make it more valuable and able to be published as a paperback. Then I published the revised version. That took a couple of days. Proves the business plan. Write short, publish the same week. And - as I mentioned – paperbacks sell better. So: upgrade in text quality, upgrade in potential earnings.)

Practice would make this faster. Generally, I can crank out an average of over 2500 words of publishable non-fiction text in a couple of hours. That's after I've finished researching, testing, and answering all my questions about a subject before starting.

Turning this production line into fiction makes the whole scene faster, as once the research is done for the settings and characters of a book, you are then pushing straight through. Unlimited stories as the characters tell you what's happening and you're just there to describe it all in text. (Yes, I proved that by testing as well – see my by-this-author link pages below this.)

The overall scene is to keep to a word-quota and schedule that doesn't burn you or your family out.

Again, this gives you the potential to earn income several times what you would make by writing longish novels.

Who knows, maybe it gets picked up for serialization on cable?

One can always dream. And any dream can be made into reality.

WRITING LINKS:

A PLOT GRID - http://calm.li/plotgrid [1]

Table of Story Structures by Robert Carlson - http://calm.li/storygridpix [2]

Vonnegut's Shapes of Stories - https://www.youtube.com/watch?v=oP3c1h8v2ZQ [3]

Six Emotional Story Arcs - http://calm.li/sixplotarcs [4]

Smashwords' Mark Coker Annual Reports - http://blog.smashwords.com/2016/04/2016survey-how-to-publish-and-sell-ebooks.html [5]

Author Earnings Reports - https://thenewpublishingstandard.com/2019/03/25/data-guys-author-earnings-report-finally-laid-rest/

K-lytics Short Stories and Short Reads Seminar - https://calm.li/K-Lytics_Short_Reads

Stephen King "On Writing" - https://books2read.com/u/m2vPR1

Lester Dent's Master Fiction Plot - http://www.paper-dragon.com/1939/dent.html [6]

Internet Movie Database - http://www.imdb.com/

---

1. http://calm.li/plotgrid

2. http://calm.li/storygridpix

3. https://www.youtube.com/watch?v=oP3c1h8v2ZQ

4. http://calm.li/sixplotarcs

5. http://blog.smashwords.com/2016/04/2016survey-how-to-publish-and-sell-ebooks.html

6. http://www.paper-dragon.com/1939/dent.html

Wikipedia - **"Binge Watching"** - https://en.wikipedia.org/wiki/Binge-watching

Wikipedia - **"Serial – Literature"** - https://en.wikipedia.org/wiki/Serial_(literature

Wikipedia - **"Soap Opera"** - https://en.wikipedia.org/wiki/Soap_opera

H. Bedford-Jones - **"This Fiction Business"** - https://calm.li/ThisFictionBusiness

Writing tactics of various authors such as Lester Dent, Algis Budrys, William Wallace Cook – **"Learning from the Pulp Masters"** - https://calm.li/LearnPulpMasters

Recommended Books You May Like

ALL OUR LATEST RELEASES[1]

Both fiction and non-fiction – each with links to major online book outlets as well as author discounts.

The Strangest Secret Library[2]

All the full references mentioned in Earl Nightingale's Strangest Secret Library available for instant download – through your online book outlet of choice or with our publisher's discount.

Books on Success and Goal Achievement[3]

Our collection of modern and classic references on how you can become a personal success and achieve your own goals – to get *everything* you want out of life.

Books on Writing & [4]Publishing[5]

Our collection of modern and classic references on how to improve your writing in our modern self-publishing age.

Speculative F[6]iction [7]Modern Parables[8]

---

1. https://livesensical.com/books/?utm_campaign=related-book-ad&utm_source=ebook

2. https://livesensical.com/book-series/

   strangest-secret-library/?utm_campaign=related-book-ad&utm_source=ebook

3. https://livesensical.com/book-series/how-to-completely-change-your-life/

4. https://livesensical.com/book-series/

   publishing-and-writing/?utm_campaign=related-book-ad&utm_source=ebook

5. https://livesensical.com/book-series/

   publishing-and-writing/?utm_campaign=related-book-ad&utm_source=ebook

Our short stories and anthologies – all in order of most recent release.

Classic Fiction[9]

Our ever-expanding collection of fiction stories that are hard to find, yet their stories never grow old. Perfect entertainment when the too-modern world becomes stale...

———————————

Visit https://livesensical.com/go/find-your-book/ to find the book you're looking for

———

6. https://livesensical.com/book-series/

   fiction/?utm_campaign=related-book-ad&utm_source=ebook

7. https://livesensical.com/book-series/

   fiction/?utm_campaign=related-book-ad&utm_source=ebook

8. https://livesensical.com/book-series/

   fiction/?utm_campaign=related-book-ad&utm_source=ebook

9. https://livesensical.com/book-series/fiction-classics/

Really Simple Writing & Publishing Series

BY DR. ROBERT C. WORSTELL

How I Survived My First Year of Fiction Writing[10]

How to Stop Feeding the Beast[11]

Author Freedom Guidebook[12]

Writing-Publishing Survival Guide[13]

Backwards Book Publishing: Save Time, Earn More, Work Less[14]

How to Write and Publish FOR FREE[15]

Cracking the Kindle Sales Code[16]

Really Simple Writing & Publishing[17]

An Honest Kindle Booksales Blueprint[18]

How to Help Librarians Love Your Book[19]

How to Write Less and Profit More[20]

---

10. https://calm.li/FIrstYearFiction

11. https://calm.li/FeedingTheBeast

12. https://calm.li/AuthorFreedom

13. https://calm.li/PublishingSurvival

14. https://calm.li/BackwardsBookPub

15. https://calm.li/PublishForFree

16. https://calm.li/CrackingKindle

17. https://calm.li/ReallySimpleWP

18. https://calm.li/KindleBlueprint

19. https://calm.li/LibrariansLove

20. https://calm.li/WriteLessProfitMore

Publish. Profit. Independence.[21]

J'APE: Just Another Publicity Excuse[22]

Writing Serial Fiction in the Real World[23]

Becoming A Writer Series

BECOMING A WRITER[24]

This Fiction Business[25]

Mystery Story Techniques for Writers[26]

Learning from the Pulp Masters[27]

How I Survived My First Year of Fiction Writing[28]

Becoming a Wealthy Writer[29]

Visit: http://calm.li/WritingPublishingRefs

21. https://calm.li/2mG93LW

22. https://calm.li/JAPE

23. https://calm.li/WritingSerialFiction

24. https://calm.li/BecomingAWriterBook

25. https://calm.li/ThisFictionBusiness

26. https://calm.li/MysteryStoryTechniques

27. https://calm.li/Pulp_Masters

28. https://calm.li/FIrstYearFiction

29. https://livesensical.com/book/becoming-a-wealthy-writer/

Becoming a Wealthy Writer Courses

A SAMPLER OF OUR EXPANDING suite of courses:

Becoming A Writer -

Dorothea Brande's original classic worked up into a readily learnable series of lessons, along with related references for download to improve the experience...

Becoming a Wealthy Writer -

Most people have a book inside them, nagging to be put into words and brought to life. And the majority of those writers who do write it, don't publish. Those few who publish seldom make a viable living from their books. Now, that can all be changed...

Author Freedom Course -

That which begins well, goes well. Learn the simple steps to acquire real freedom in your writing and publishing. A very frank and simple series of steps so you can get started today – with only what you already have at hand.

Backwards Book Publishing -

Books, in all their versions, are idea containers. The trick to leveraging these is to work backward from the most profitable container, the non-fiction course...

Write Less, Profit More -

How writing short stories – a traditional starting place for many writers – enables you to learn your craft faster, and create more outlets for income meanwhile...

https://livesensical.com/go/becomingawritercourses/

Don't Miss Out...

Who Else Wants to Write Bestsellers

That Become Classics?

Get No-Charge Access to

Writing and Publishing Materials

from Our Library Collection

Instant Access – Join Here

Click or type into your browser:

http://livesensical.com/go/writingbooks/

Did You Like This Book?

Did you love *Writing Serial Fiction In the Real World 2.0*? Then you should read *How I Survived My First Year of Fiction Writing*[2] by Dr. Robert C. Worstell!

Writing Fiction isn't very hard - *if you throw out 95% of what you've been taught is true.*

Academics and those who earn their income marketing how-to books and courses, as well as freelance editors, proofreaders, and cover designers all have a vested interest in making it seem that writing and publishing is very difficult.

It's just not true at all.

Yes, there is a lot of hard work to it. And it's not something you can learn overnight. And you have to keep studying and practicing your craft to get any good at it - just as musicians and athletes practice daily.

---

2. https://books2read.com/u/bO6EyW

3. https://books2read.com/u/bO6EyW

But you can publish your first book on Amazon in a half hour from now. It's that simple. (Of course you can use a pen name to avoid being embarassed later.)

The point is that writing and publishing is simple, and inexpensive.

Here's the secret: **Write short and narrow, publish long and wide.**

Write short stories for a specific sub-genre you like to read.

Publish long in advance (pre-schedule) and wide to every possible outlet - including free ones like Wattpad and Medium.

Including setting up all the accounts, you can publish everywhere on the globe in an afternoon. For no cost, except your time.

This book is a compilation of the blog posts I wrote and published while I was busy doing a test of everything I'd rounded up and studied about writing and publishing fiction.

And it's a very raw, passionate description of exactly what I found works - as I was testing it.

So it's more an adventure that starts from having no published fiction and ends up with have well over a hundred books published. Step by step, blow by blow.

To test what I'd found and bring it all to you.

Scroll Up and Get Your Copy Now.

Read more at https://livesensical.com/book-author/ dr-robert-c-worstell/.

Also by Dr. Robert C. Worstell

Change Your Life Toolset
Get Your Self Scam Free

Make Yourself Great Again Library
Why You Got All That Stuff
The Art of Wonk, Compleat

Masters of Copywriting
Breakthrough Copywriter 2.0: An Advertising Field Guide to Eugene
M. Schwartz' Classic

Mindset Stacking Guides
Make Yourself Great Again Part 1
Make Yourself Great Again Part 2
Make Yourself Great Again Part 3
Make Yourself Great Again Part 4
Choose. Believe. Win.
Make Yourself Great Again - Complete Collection

Go Thunk Yourself, Again!

PMA Science of Success
Napoleon Hill's PMA: Science of Success Course - An Introduction

Really Simple Writing & Publishing
How To Write And Publish For Free
Backwards Book Publishing: Save Time, Earn More, Work Less
Writing-Publishing Survival Guide
Author Freedom Guidebook
How to Stop Feeding the Beast
A Completely Unauthorized Instafreebie Guidebook
How I Survived My First Year of Fiction Writing
How to Become an Instant Author in 30 Seconds
Becoming a Wealthy Writer
Marketers & Writers - Scammers & Dupes
How to Write Less and Profit More - Version 2.0
Writing Serial Fiction In the Real World 2.0

Standalone
Farm Less, Profit More: Lessons in Regenerative Grazing

Watch for more at https://livesensical.com/book-author/
dr-robert-c-worstell/.

Midwest Journal Press
Finding You Books that Continue to Change Your Life

About the Publisher

"Finding you books that continue to change your life."

A veteran publishing imprint and a practical philosophy for life, Midwest Journal Press has been active publishing new and established authors since 2006.

We take advantage of the new Print on Demand and ebook technologies to enable wider discovery for authors.

We publish in most of the major genres of fiction and non-fiction.

Our current emphasis is in speculative fiction modern parables.

For More Information, Visit:

https://livesensical.com/midwestjournalpress/